MORALS STOP QUARRELS!

Lessons with

Jordan and Kenly

Authored By

Dr. Deshawn Rouse

PATASKITY PUBLISHING CO.

Pataskity Publishing Co.
207 Hudson Trce Suite 102
Augusta, GA 30907
pataskitypublishing.com
(706) 250-3956

Dedication

I dedicate this book to my sons Tarique, Jeremiah, Kenly, and Jordan. I also dedicate this book to my goddaughter, Destiny. I love you all, and each of you bring a unique perspective to my life that amazes me.

Particularly, to Kenly and Jordan, I would like to say that because you are the younger sons. The past few years have been a complete joy watching you two grow and mature into handsome and strong men. When God gave me you guys, he knew exactly what he was doing. Best friends for life, love you!

Contents

Leaving from Mother
Golf Cart

"*Don't ride around the yard in the golf cart too fast without looking around!*" I told Jordan.

On this particular day, Jordan was zooming through the yard on the golf cart. All I heard was sounds of *zoom, zoom, zoom,* and looking back at his brother Kenly who was chasing him.

"**CRASH!**" While looking back, Jordan drove the golf cart into a light pole in the yard.

The golf cart hit the light pole, and the back two wheels pushed the cart and made it stand up straight on the pole!

"Jordan, what have you done?"
I asked angrily.

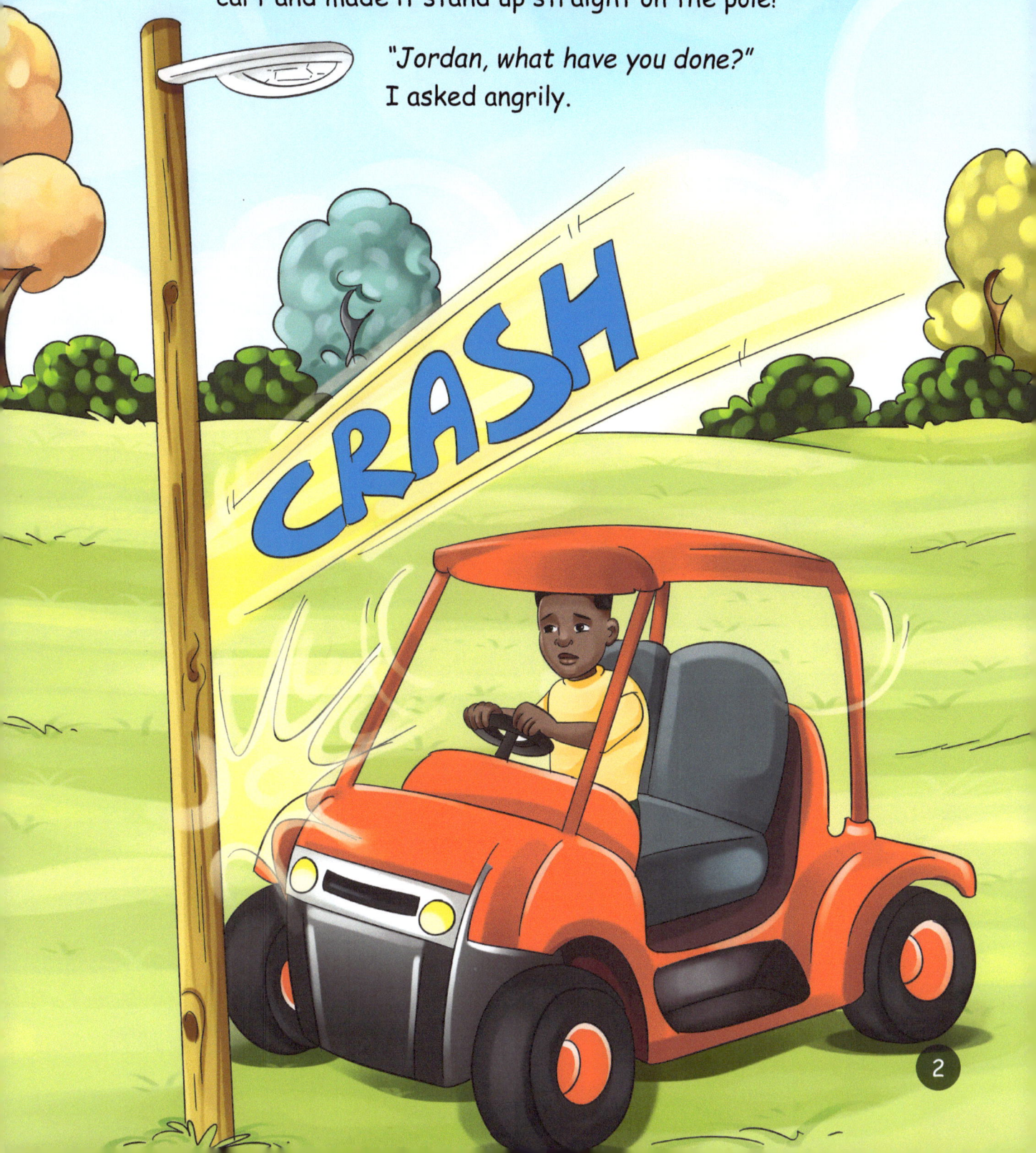

CRASH

Personally, I knew that Jordan was really scared. After seeing that he was okay, and the golf cart had no damage, I decided instead of yelling and punishment to turn this into a teachable moment to learn a valuable moral. I called everyone outside. We took pictures and laughed at this crazy accident.

"What lesson did you learn, Jordan?" I asked.

Jordan replied and said, *"To listen to instructions and to be aware of my surroundings."*

I then told him, *"Good job, I am proud of you because it is important to be obedient and listening is a moral. Remember, a moral will stop a quarrel."*

Game

Kenly and Jordan were always taught not to make each other angry! However, on this particular day, Kenly and Jordan were playing a game and on this particular day Kenly was losing.

Not wanting to see the outcome of the game, Kenly reached over and unplugged the game which immediately stopped.

"Kenly, I hate you!" I heard. So, I ran to the room.

"Hey you two, what did I tell you about this?" I asked.

While both were arguing their point, I became mad.

I had to discover a better way to diffuse this anger and shouting.

After sitting them down and calming myself, I began to have a teachable moment and discuss an important moral.

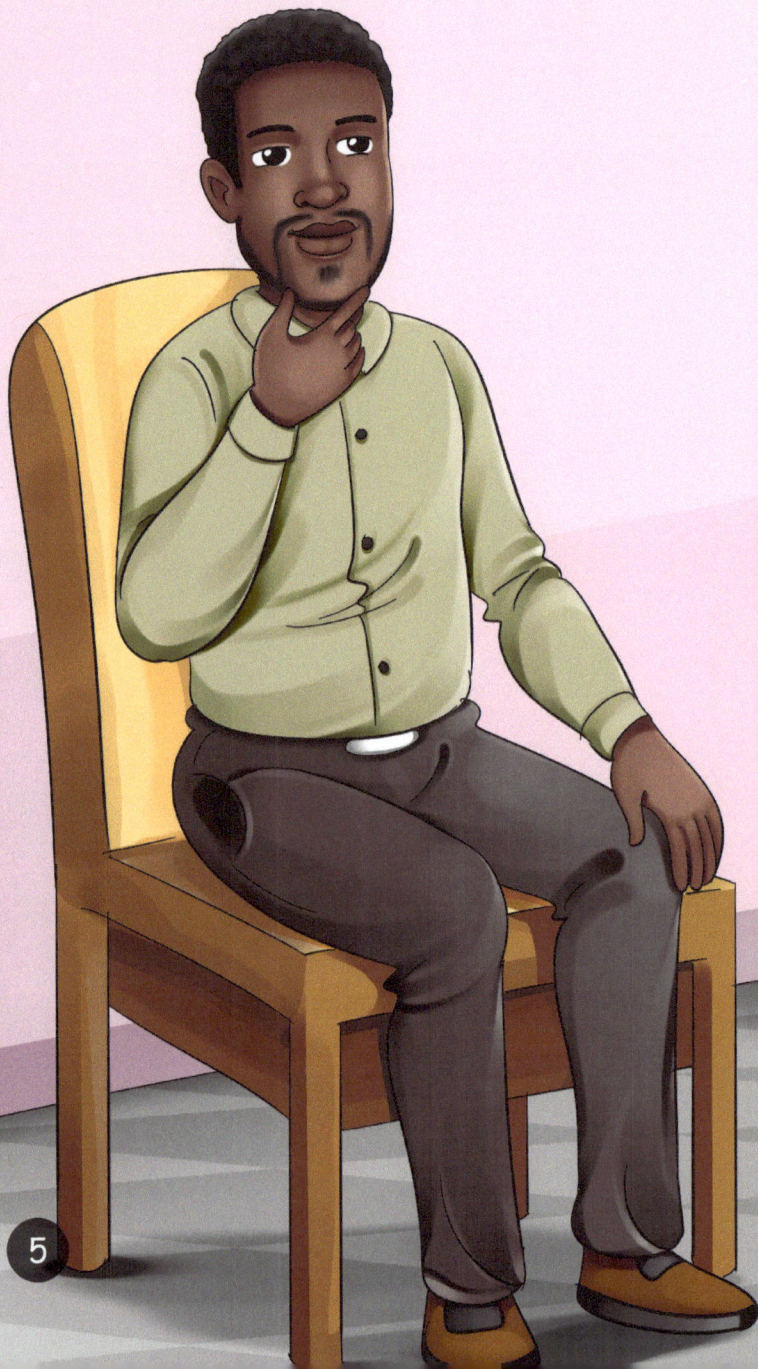

"Kenly, would you want someone to take something from you when you were almost finished with it?" I asked. "No sir." He replied.

"Jordan, would you want someone to tell you that they hate you? What awful words!"

"No sir." He replied. Then I said to him, "Now cut the game on and play again. If you lose, it is just a game. Sometimes in life you may not win, but that does not mean you shut it off! Losing does not mean that you are a loser.

At some point, you will lose something or someone that you once had. You may lose a sports game. This valuable moral is to still smile, and continue to show morals of endurance, patience and meekness. These morals will always stop quarrels!"

6

Sharing

One day I was in the store and Jordan was with me. Jordan, who had just got his allowance, decided to buy himself and Kenly a pizza, chips and a drink.

After returning home, Jordan surprised Kenly with his pizza, chips, and drink.

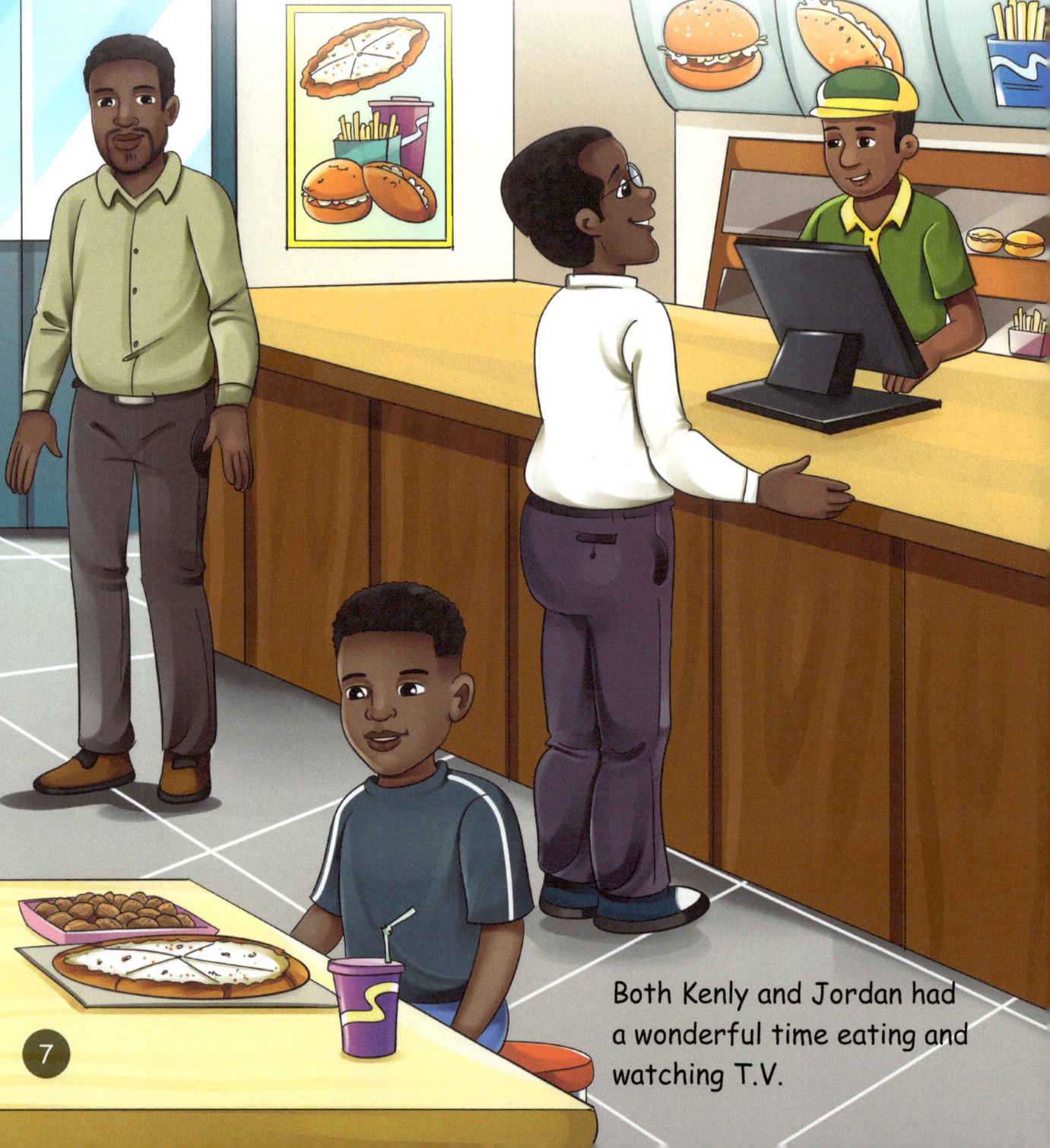

Both Kenly and Jordan had a wonderful time eating and watching T.V.

A few days later, I had to go back to the store and this time Kenly was with me. While shopping, Kenly decided to buy him a pizza, chips, and a drink but I noticed that he did not get anything for his brother.

I asked Kenly, "Are you going to get Jordan something since he thought about you the other day?" "No!" I was shocked at his response. "Why not?"

He said, "*This is my money and I want to spend it just on me.*" While he was right that it was his money, I needed to make this another teachable moment.

Your little brother loves you so much that he wanted you to enjoy what he had while you guys watched T.V. It would be nice if you thought about him the same way he thought about you instead of being focused on "this is my money."

"Have you ever thought that if we saw you genuinely sharing, that your mother and I would give you more?" He looked as if he was really thinking about it.

"I'm sorry dad. I see what you mean." So, he grabbed his brother the same thing and they had a really great time the rest of the day eating and sharing. Sharing is a lifelong moral because when you share, it shows how much you care.

Missing Money

One day, I was counting money at the kitchen table and it was about five hundred dollars that I had reserved for bills.

Prior to that, Jordan really wanted a new video game, and he begged me repeatedly for the money to get it. Every time he asked, I would say "*wait*" or "*I'll get it soon*," anything to just get him to calm down and not ask me again.

A few days later, I paid the bills but something was not matching up. I was simply thinking that I miscounted. I thought nothing of it until one day Kenly ran through the door with a mysterious piece of mail.

"*Jordan won, Jordan won!*" with excitement Kenly said.

I heard him but I thought little of it until my oldest son came from work and said, "*Dad, did you hear the good news about Jordan?*"

I asked, "*What?*"

He said, "*Jordan won some money for registering in an online game.*" I called for Jordan and he came with the mail.

On the first look I knew something was wrong. He said that he did not open it yet but it was opened, and in a plain envelope with no return address. What really was strange was that it said on the front of the envelope, "Jordan you won 150.00$," and it was all written in pencil with crooked letters.

"Wait a minute!" I said.

"There is no way that someone is going to mail 150.00$ in an envelope with no return address and say on the front, 'Jordan you won 150.00$' in pencil with crooked letters!"

After pressing him several times and he began laughing, I knew I had to turn this into a positive. I asked, "So Jordan, did you take the money that I was counting the other day at the table?"

"Yes sir," he replied. I explained to him that you never have to steal to get what you want; all you have to do is be patient and you will get it. I told him that I apologize for putting him off for so long by telling him that I will get it over and over again.

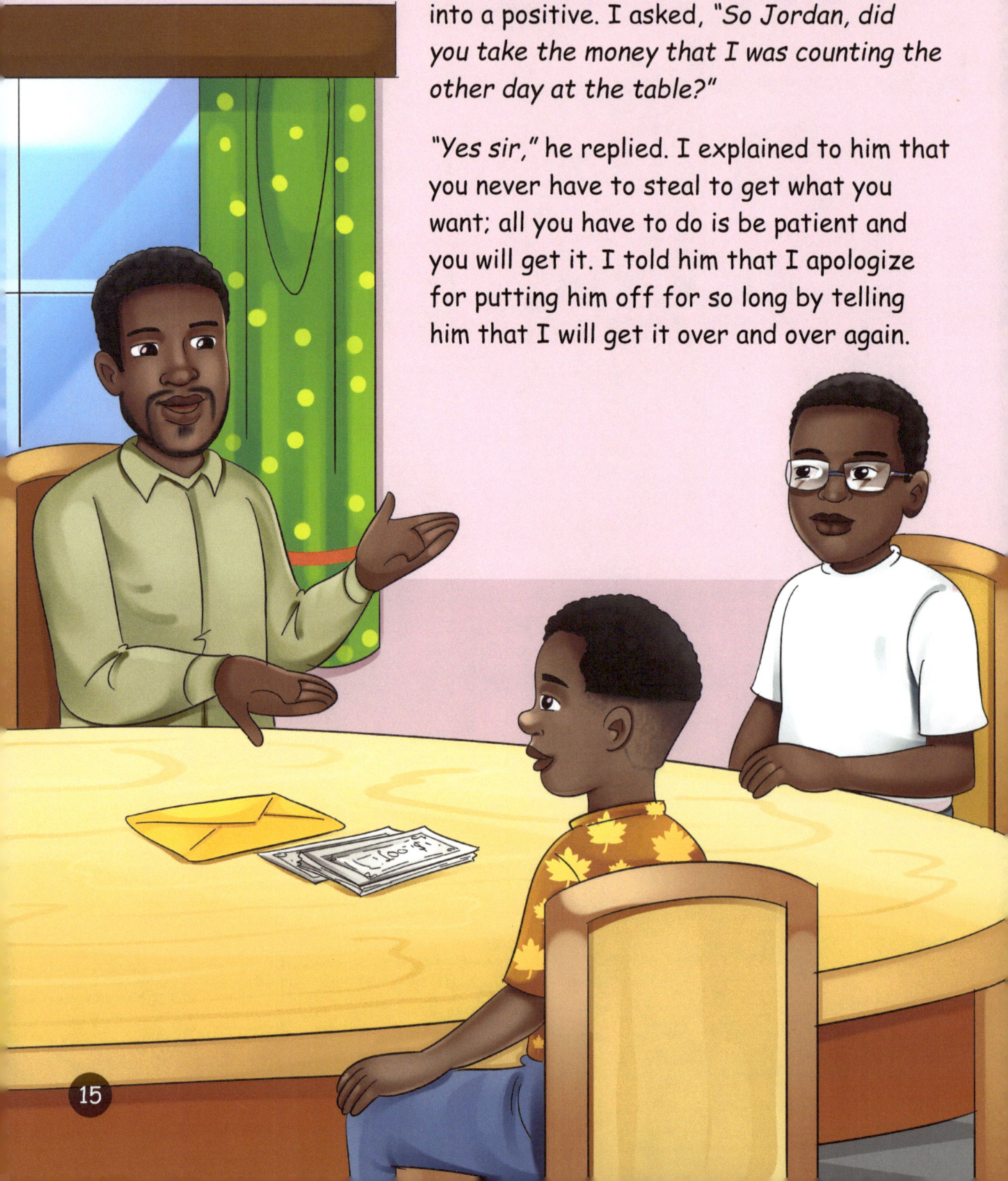

We both learned a lesson that day. For me: Do not promise someone something and fail to follow through with it and for that person. For him: Do not take things that do not belong to you. Be patient for if it is not done today, it will eventually be done. These types of morals will stop any future quarrels!

Rock

One day, I was on the front porch reading several magazines. Kenly was in the driveway playing next to the truck. Kenly was pretending to play school and he was the teacher. It sounded to me that Kenly was having a good time.

I became captivated by what I was reading, then I heard a streaking sound. I heard it several times, but it did not register with me until something in my head said, "look up!"

When I looked up, I was shocked! There Kenly was with a rock in his hand and using the passenger side door of our vehicle as a chalk board for his imaginary class.

I saw three long streaks. "Oh no, stop! Stop!" I yelled.

This was funny to Kenly, and grabbing his hand, I shook the rock away from it. I was highly upset. I knew spanking was not right while I was angry. I calmed myself down and made this a teachable moment.

"Kenly, you can't mark up the truck," I explained. When you do things like this, you are costing us money that we could use for something else, and now we have to get the truck repainted. Do you understand?

"Yes," he said and I am sorry. Kids usually play with and throw rocks and I guess it was my time to learn. I should have told him about the dangers and temptations of rocks earlier but now was our teachable time. An important moral is to always value and take care of what you have in life.

Rock and Window

On another day after being warned about the degree of rocks, I was on the lawn mower cutting the yard. I recall Jordan was in the driveway playing behind the truck.

After a long evening of cutting in the area where the truck was, I was extremely exhausted. I noticed that the back window was shattered. Then, I got off the lawn mower to go closer to examine it.

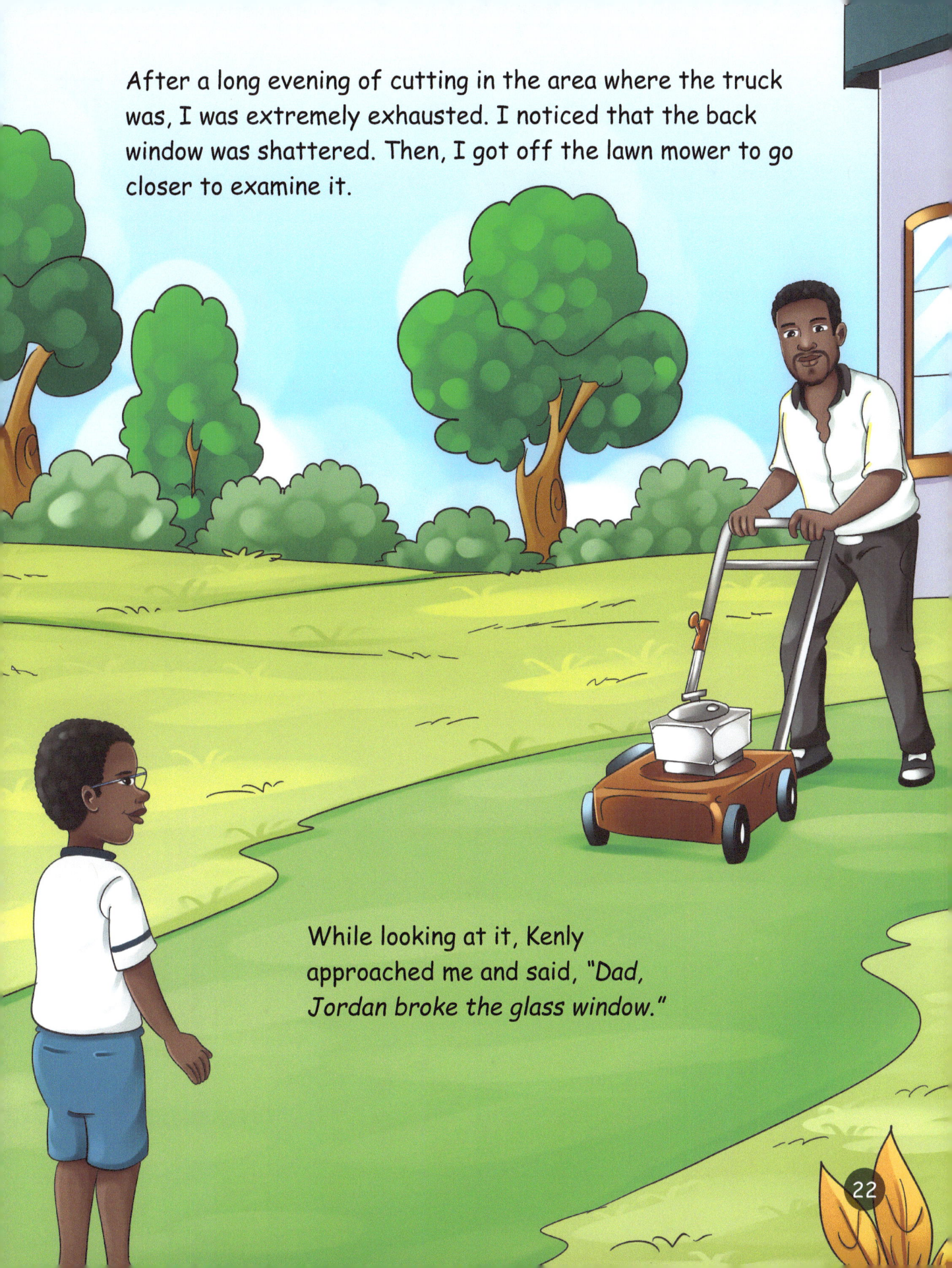

While looking at it, Kenly approached me and said, "Dad, Jordan broke the glass window."

I told him to tell Jordan to come here and I was furious. Jordan came with the look of fear on his face; "*Sir?*" he asked.

"*Did you break the window?*" I asked.

Looking at me scared, he said, "*Yes sir.*" I said,
"*Why didn't you tell me? You had me thinking
that I did it?*" He began to explain why he
was throwing rocks up, and he mistakenly threw
one backwards and it shattered the window.

Jordan said, "I was too scared to tell you, and I did not want to get in trouble."

Realizing that this could be a teachable moment, I said to Jordan, "You knew what I told you about rocks. I do not want you to feel that if you ever did something you could not tell me. We all deserve a second chance."

Boy, was he relieved and I felt as if I was a person that he could come to if he ever did something wrong!

A moral that will always stop a quarrel is to teach yourself, "We all deserve a second chance because no one is perfect!"

Get Ready

It is a school morning. Kenly and Jordan are getting ready for school. "Get ready Jordan," Kenly said repeatedly. After about the 7th time, I went to check on the situation.

There was Jordan with his pants, shirt, and socks on with no shoes; however, Kenly had only dressed in a shirt so far.

I asked him, "Why aren't you ready yet?" He began to say that he was trying to keep Jordan on track.

"But it is almost time for you guys to go and because you are so focused on Jordan, you are not ready," I said. He explained again that he wanted Jordan to be ready. I could see that he was missing the point.

I slowed everything down, and explained that while it is a good thing that he wanted Jordan to stay on track, it would also be smart to exemplify what you want others to be doing. If you want someone to do something then be the example for them, and that way you will not be making others do something that you are not doing. From that day on, Kenly's behavior regarding leading got better!

A moral to always remember is to lead by example. If you want a follower, do what you teach others!

Clothes

Clothes, clothes, clothes! It is that time again! The clothes have been washed and it is now time to fold. That is the chore for Kenly and Jordan, and it can be a bit challenging.

"My basket, no my basket!" "I'll do white! No, I'll do dark!" is the way it goes.

This can often go on for long periods of time with nothing getting accomplished.

"Hey, you two!" I would usually exclaim! I want you two to work together.

I do not want either of you to say, "I don't want to do it with him". Even when Jordan and Kenley work together on this specific task, the clothes usually take a lifetime to get separated and they never, ever get put away!

I always motivate them to get them to see the benefit of working together. Guys when you work together, you can usually do it faster and put it away quicker.

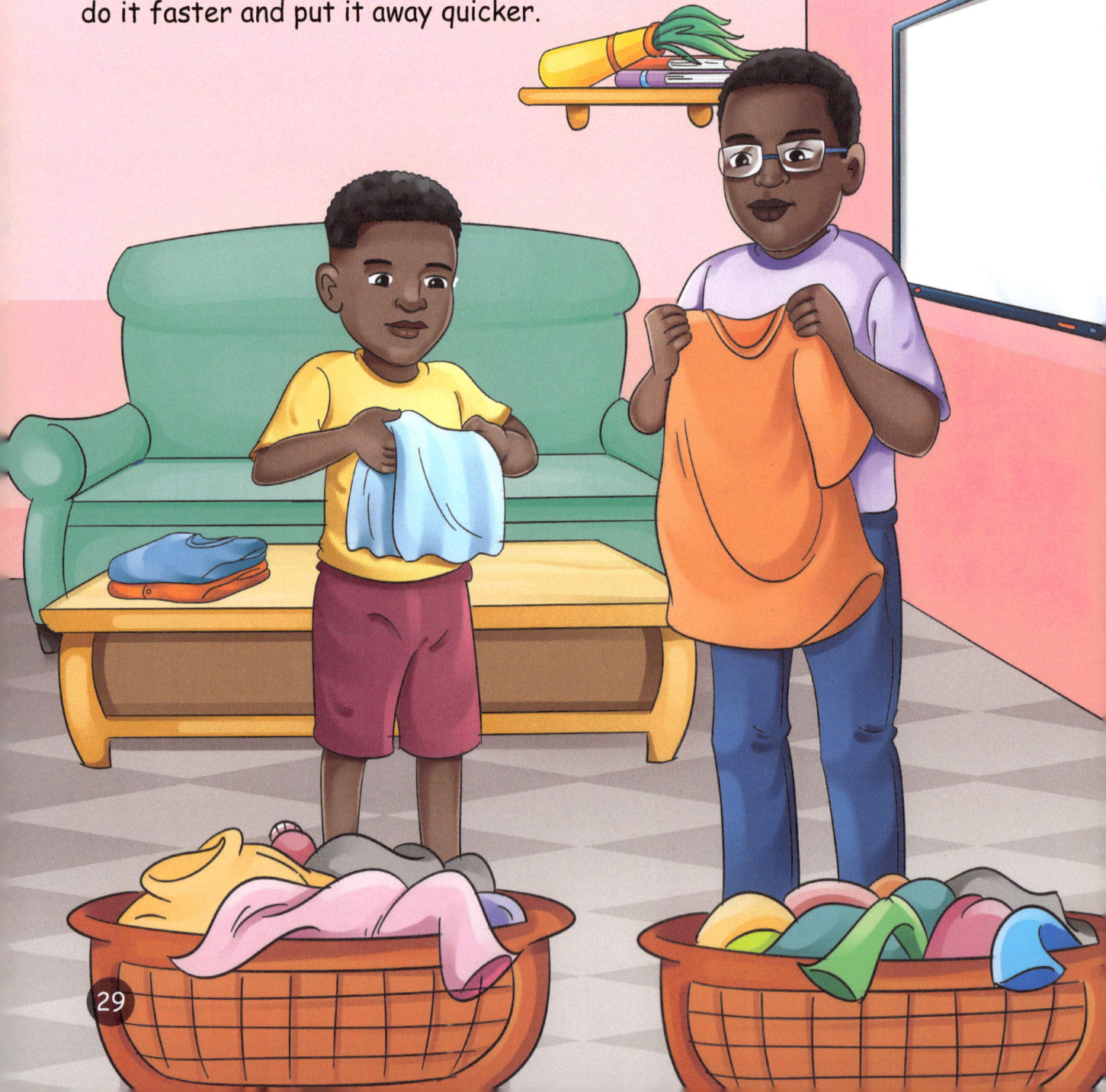

"Wouldn't you like to hurry up and finish, so that you can move on to something else or go and do what you want to do?"

"Yes," they replied.

After trying it, the two not only saw how smoothly working together is, but also they enjoyed completing the chore together.

"See, you two, in this life you will have to learn to work with others and even though you will sometimes still do it separately, you still need to know that an important life skill is cooperating. Cooperation and collaboration are morals that will stop quarrels."

Cleaning Up

The dishes are piling up, and the carpet needs vacuuming. This is usually the time that you can see frowned faces and hear abrupt sighs. *"I do not want to do it."* This is sometimes the response. *"We did it the other day"* is another familiar response.

"You two, let's not make this hard," I would often say as I wondered, *"How can I get them to see the importance of cleaning up without getting frustrated?"*

I sat them down and explained that we have a beautiful home. It is up to us, and us only to keep it up. "Do you love your home?" I would ask, and the answer was, "Yes."

If you keep it nice and clean, then when guests come over, you would not have to feel ashamed like you should have done better.

Also, if you do things this way, simple household tasks will be much easier. When you keep things regularly clean, you help out everyone else. When they do it, they help you too as well.

Just like you want a nice clean hotel room when you visit a hotel, let us treat our home the same way. There they go, them two, washing dishes, vacuuming, dusting, mopping and spraying air freshener.

There I am with my feet up drinking my drink while relaxing. "*Thanks guys!*" I said excitedly and finally appreciatively. The moral is to always teach your children life-long morals!

www.ingramcontent.com/pod-product-compliance
Lightning Source LLC
Chambersburg PA
CBHW041704200326
41518CB00027B/177